gone before us

praying for the dead

compiled by
Stephen Joseph Wolf

in the morning	page 3
at daytime	pg 16
in the evening	pg 23
at bedtime	pg 33
in the middle of the night	pg 39

www.idjc.org

dedicated to

Will D. Campbell, the Baptist Preacher
who helped me get to know Mr. Jesus,
&
Edward Alberts, Catholic Pastor,
vicar of liquor and friend,

whose June 2013 deaths finally prompted
this long-considered compilation

Gone Before Us:
Praying for the Dead
Copyright © 2016, 2023
Stephen Joseph Wolf
All rights reserved. No part of this book may be copied or reproduced in any form or by any means without the written permission of the publisher, except for the inclusion of brief quotations in a review, or for personal use as described below.

The psalms and canticles are slightly altered from the meditation rendering in *Rainbow Psalms in 30 Days*. The choices made in this meditation rendering are available at idjc.org, except that "The LORD" is used here instead of the Hebrew "Adonai" for the divine name.

The songs, previously published in *Hinge Hour Singer*, are understood by the publisher to be in the public domain. Original text and music for most of the songs are available at www.nethymnal.org.

Gone Before Us is intended for private prayer
and is not approved for public liturgy.

printed and distributed by Ingram
published by IDJC press
www.idjc.org.

ISBN 978-1-937081-51-5

E book 978-937081-76-8

morning

Sing with all the saints in glo-ry,
Sing the res-ur-rec-tion song!
Death and sor-row, earth's dark sto-ry,
To the for-mer days be-long.
All a-round the clouds are/ break-ing,
Soon the/ storms of time shall cease;
In God's im-age we, a-wa-king,
Know the ev-er-last-ing peace.

O what glo-ry, far ex-ceed-ing
All that eye has yet per-ceived!
Ho-liest hearts, for a-ges plead-ing,
Nev-er that full joy con-ceived.
God has prom-ised, Christ pre/-pares it,
There on/ high our wel-come waits.
Ev-'ry hum-ble spir-it shares it;
Christ has passed th'e-ter-nal gates.

#69, Text: William J. Irons, 1873
Music: 8787D, HYMN TO JOY, Ludwig van Beethoven, 1770,
adapted by Edward Hodges, 1827
Popular melody for *Joyful Joyful We Adore You*

Psalm 51

Antiphon *Bones that have been crushed*
shall leap for joy before the Lord.

Have mercy on me, God,
in accord with your unfailing love;
in accord with your great compassion
blot out my transgressions.

Wash me of my many iniquities
and cleanse me from my sin,
for I know my transgressions
and my sin is before me always.

Against you yourself I sinned;
doing what is bad in your eyes.
You are proven right when you speak
and justified when you judge.
Surely we are sinners from birth,
from conception in a mother's womb.

Surely you desire truth in our inner parts;
in my inmost place you teach me wisdom.
You cleanse me with hyssop
and I will be clean;
you wash me
and I will be whiter than snow…

You let me hear joy and gladness;
let the bones you let be crushed now rejoice.
Hide your faces from my sins
and blot out all my iniquities.

A clean heart create in me, God!
Renew inside me a spirit to be steadfast.
Do not cast me from your presences,
nor take from me your Holy Spirit.

Restore to me the joy of your salvation
and sustain in me a willing spirit.
I will teach transgressors your ways
and sinners will turn back to you.

Save me from bloodguilt, God,
God of my salvation;
my tongue will sing of your justice.
Lord, open my lips
and my mouth will proclaim your praise.

Sacrifices give you no delight;
I could bring a burnt offering,
but it would give you no pleasure.
The sacrifices, God, you will not despise
are a broken spirit and a contrite heart.

Psalm 51, continued

Make Zion prosper in your pleasure,
and build up the walls of Jerusalem.
You will delight in the sacrifice of the just,
burnt offerings and whole offerings,
bulls offered on your altar.

*Glory to the Father, and to the Son,
and to the Holy Spirit*

As it was in the beginning, is now,
and will be for ever. Amen.

Antiphon *Bones that have been crushed
shall leap for joy before the Lord.*

Isaiah 38:10-14,17b-20

Antiphon *At the threshold of death,*
rescue me, Lord.

I asked, "Must I go in the prime of my days
through the gates of Sheol;
must I be robbed of the rest of my years?"

I said, "I will no longer see the LORD,
the LORD in the land of the living.
As a dweller of the place of cessation
I will look on humanity no longer."

My house was pulled down
and taken from me
like the tent of my shepherd;
I rolled up my life,
as a weaver cuts off from a loom.

From day to night you made an end of me.
I waited till dawn;
all my bones are broken as by a lion.
From day to night you made an end of me.

Like a swift or thrush I cried;
I moaned like the dove.
My eyes to the heavens grew weak.
Lord, troubles are at me; come to my aid…

Isaiah 38:10-14,17b-20, continued

In your love you have kept my self
out of the pit of destruction;
indeed you put behind your back
all my sins.

Sheol cannot praise you
and death cannot sing to you praise,
nor can those going down the pit
hope for your faithfulness.

The living alive praise you,
as I do this day.
Fathers and mothers tell the children
all about your faithfulness.

The LORD saves us;
we will play our stringed instruments
and sing in the temple of the LORD
all the days of our lives.

> *Glory to the Father, and to the Son,*
> *and to the Holy Spirit*
>
> As it was in the beginning, is now,
> and will be for ever. Amen.

Antiphon *At the threshold of death,*
rescue me, Lord.

Psalm 146

Antiphon *I will sing praise to God all my life.*

Hallelujah! Praise the LORD, my soul!
I will praise the LORD during my life,
I will sing praise to my God while I still am.

Trust neither royalty nor human beings
in whom there is no salvation.
Their spirit-breath departs,
and they return to the ground.
On that day their plans come to nothing.

Blessed are they whose help is Jacob's God,
whose hope and God are the LORD,
the maker of heaven and earth
and the sea and all that is in them.

The one staying faithful to forever
defends justice for the oppressed
and gives food to the hungry.

The LORD sets prisoners free;
The LORD gives sight to the blind;
The LORD lifts those who are bowed down;
The LORD loves the just.

Psalm 146, continued

The LORD watches over alien strangers,
and sustains the orphan and the widow,
but frustrates the ways that are bad.

The LORD reigns to forever, your God, Zion,
from generation to generation.
Hallelujah! Praise the LORD!

> *Glory to the Father, and to the Son,*
> *and to the Holy Spirit*
>
> As it was in the beginning, is now,
> and will be for ever. Amen.

Antiphon   *I will sing praise to God all my life.*

READING   **1 Thessalonians 4:13-18**

Brothers and sisters, we do not wish you to be unaware about the ones who have fallen asleep, lest you grieve as the rest who have no hope. For if we believe that Jesus died and rose again, so also will God bring through Jesus the ones who have fallen asleep.

MORNING

For we say this to you by a word of the Lord that we who are alive even to the coming of the Lord may by no means precede the ones already asleep.

The Lord himself with a commanding word and a voice of an archangel and with a trumpet of God, will come from heaven and the dead in Christ will rise first. Then we who are alive will be caught up together with them in the clouds to a meeting of the Lord in the air.

And so shall we be with the Lord always. Console one another with these words.

Responsory   Psalm 30

I will praise you, Lord;
 - *for you have rescued me.*

You turned my sorrow into joy,
 - *for you have rescued me.*

Glory to the Father, and to the Son,
and to the Holy Spirit.
 - *I will praise you, Lord, for you have rescued me.*

CANTICLE OF ZECHARIAH   **Luke 1:68-79**

Antiphon
John 11:25,26
I am the resurrection and the life;
one believing in me
will live even in dying
and everyone living and believing in me
does not ever die.

In Easter
Season
The splendor of the Risen Christ
shines on all the people
redeemed by his blood, alleluia.

+ Blessed be the Lord the God of Israel
who chose a people to visit with redemption,
and raised salvation in the house of David,
saving strength from God's own servant,

speaking from the age of the prophets
through the mouth of the holy prophet:
Salvation out of enmity,
even out of those who hate us,

to show our ancestors how mercy works, -
and to remember the holy promise of the Lord,
the covenant made for our ancestor Abraham,
calming our fear and making us free
to serve with holy justice
    before God all our days.

And you also child -
will be called a prophet of the Most High
for you will go before the Lord
> to prepare his way
and give to people a knowledge of salvation
known in accepting forgiveness of their sins.

From the tender mercy of our God,
the sun rising from the height
> will visit with light
for those who sit in the dark
> or shadow of death,
and to guide our feet into the way of peace.

*Glory to the Father, and to the Son,
and to the Holy Spirit*

As it was in the beginning, is now,
and will be for ever. Amen.

Antiphon	*I am the resurrection and the life;*
John 11:25,26	*one believing in me*
	will live even in dying
	and everyone living and believing in me
	does not ever die.
In Easter	*The splendor of the Risen Christ*
Season	*shines on all the people*
	redeemed by his blood, alleluia.

INTERCESSIONS

God and Father of us all,
as you created us in your image,
> - *so bring us alive into your presence
> and help us be fully alive here on earth.*

You have fed us with bread from heaven;
> - *prepare us for the heavenly banquet
> even as you give us our daily bread.*

You sent an angel of mercy
to comfort your Son in his agony;
> - *cover with consolations all who mourn.*

You saved the three youths
from the fiery furnace;
> - *free your people who suffer from sin.*

God, as you raised Jesus from the dead,
> - *raise all your sons and daughters
> who have gone before us.*

Eternal rest grant unto him/her/them, O Lord,
> - *and let perpetual light shine upon him/her/them.*

May he/she/they rest in peace.
> - *Amen.*

MORNING 15

May his/her/their soul(s)
and the souls of all the faithful departed
through the mercy of God rest in peace.
  - *Amen.*

And may the peace of God
which is beyond all human understanding
keep our minds and hearts
in the knowledge and love of God and of the Son,
our Lord and Savior Jesus Christ.
  - *Amen.*

> **Our Fa-ther**, who art in heav-en,
> hal-lowed be thy name.
> Thy king-dom come,
> thy will be done
> on earth as it is in heav-en.
> Give us this day our dai-ly bread
> and for-give us our tres-pass-es,
> as we for-give those
> who tres-pass a-gainst/ us,
> and lead us not in-to temp-ta/-tion,
> but de-liv-er us from e\-vil.

+ May the Lord bless us,
  protect us from all evil,
  and bring us to everlasting life.   ***Amen.***

daytime

Song text: from the Beatitudes in Matthew 5:1-12
Music: 8888 LM, OLD HUNDREDTH, Louis Bourgeois,
first published in *Genevan Psalter*, 1551
Popular melody for ***Praise God From Whom All Blessings Flow***

Bless-ed are you in spir-it poor,
held down in heav-y pov-er-ty
in full de-pend-ence on the Lord;
yours is the roy-al realm of God.

And bless-ed too are you who mourn,
who shed the tears of hu-man grief;
they hon-or loss a-mid the pain;
re-mem-ber love, you'll laugh a-gain.

Bless-ed are you who join the meek
em-brac-ing risk to fol-low Christ;
mind, bod-y, soul, and will-ing strength,
in-her-it ho-ly land at length.

You bless-ed hun-gry, you who thirst:
with thirst and hun-ger sat-is-fied
in right-eous fair-ness, jus-tice due,
gen-u-ine joy in grat-i-tude.

And bless-ed you who mer-cy show,
re-ceived in mea-sure giv-en well:
the great-est gift of Je-sus Christ,
so wise are all who claim this prize.

Bless-ed are you, the clean of heart,
in sing-le fo-cus on the good,
who live in free-dom blem-ish free,
your cen-ter, God, whom you shall see.

And bless-ed you who seek for peace
be-yond what hu-mans un-der-stand
in pa-tient prayer and lis-ten-ing,
as sons and daugh-ters of the King.

Re-joice in glad-ness, last-ing joy,
who for the sake of what is right
bear per-se-cu-tion for the good,
dwell safe-ly in the realm of God.

Psalm 70

Antiphon   *Look on me, Lord, with loving kindness
and come to my rescue.*

God, come to save me;
LORD, make haste to help me!
May plans to seek my life
be shamed and confused;

Psalm 70, continued

> May the desire for my ruin
> be turned back in disgrace
> and ones saying "aha!" turn back in shame.
>
> May all who seek you rejoice and be glad
> and may lovers of salvation say always,
> "Let God be exalted."
>
> Yet I am poor and needy, God,
> come to me quickly and do not delay,
> LORD, my help and my deliverer.

Glory to the Father, and to the Son, and to the Holy Spirit

As it was in the beginning, is now, and will be for ever. Amen.

Antiphon   *Look on me, Lord, with loving kindness and come to my rescue.*

Psalm 85

Antiphon   *Lay hands, Lord, onto the wounds of sin.*

> You showed favor, LORD, to your land;
> you restored the fortune of Jacob.
> You forgave the iniquity of your people;
> you pardoned all of their sin.
> You set aside all of your wrath;
> you turned from your fierce anger.

Restore us, God of our salvation!
And put away your displeasure toward us.
Will you be angry with us to forever?
Will you prolong your anger
to generation and generation?

Will you not revive us again
that your people may rejoice in you?
Show us, LORD, your unfailing love
and grant us your salvation.

I will listen to what my LORD God will say
promising peace to the people,
even to the saints,
but not letting them return to folly.
Surely near to those in awe is their salvation,
the glory to dwell in our land.

Love and Fidelity meet;
Justice and Peace kiss.
Fidelity springs forth from the earth
and Justice looks down from the heavens.

Indeed the LORD will give the good
and our land will yield her harvest,
Justice going forward to prepare the way
for the steps of the Lord.

Psalm 85, continued

Glory to the Father, and to the Son, and to the Holy Spirit

As it was in the beginning, is now, and will be for ever. Amen.

Antiphon   *Lay hands, Lord, onto the wounds of sin.*

Psalm 86

Antiphon   *Grant strength, Lord, to your servant,
and save the child of your maidservant!*

LORD, hear in your ear;
answer me for I am poor and needy.
Guard my life for I am devoted;
save your servant, my God,
the one trusting in you.

Have mercy on me, Lord,
for to you I call all the day.
Bring joy to your servant,
for to you, Lord, I lift up my soul.

Indeed, Lord, you are kind and forgiving
and abundant in love for all who call to you.
LORD, hear my prayer;
listen to the sound of my cries for mercy.

In the day of my trouble I will call to you
for you will answer me…
There is none like you among so-called "gods"
and there are no deeds like yours, Lord.

All the nations you made will come
and they will worship before you, Lord,
and they will bring glory to your name
for you are great and do marvelous deeds,
you, God, you yourself.

LORD, teach me your way
and I will walk in your truth.
Undivide my heart
that I may revere your name.

I will praise you, Lord my God,
with all my heart
and I will glorify your name to forever
for great is your love of me
and you deliver my soul
from the depth of Sheol.

Arrogant ones attack against me, God;
a band of ruthless people seek my life
and do not regard you before them.

Psalm 86, continued

But you, Lord God,
Compassionate and Gracious,
slow of anger, and abundant in love and fidelity:
Turn to me! And have mercy on me!

Grant your strength to your servant
and save the child of your handservant!
Give to me a sign of goodness
that enmity may see and find shame,
for you, LORD, help me and comfort me.

Glory to the Father, and to the Son, and to the Holy Spirit
As it was in the beginning, is now, and will be for ever. Amen.

Antiphon *Grant strength, Lord, to your servant,*
and save the child of your maidservant!

READING **Wisdom of Solomon 1:13,14a,15**

God did not make death and takes no delight in the destruction of the living; God fashioned all things that they might have being.

Justice does not die.

Responsory Psalm 23

When I walk in the deep dark valley, I will not fear,
  - *For you, Lord, are with me.*

Let us bless the Lord. ***Thanks be to God.***

evening

I know that my Re/-deem-er\ lives;
What com-fort this sweet sen-tence gives!
Liv-ing, my Proph/-et/, Priest\, and\ King;
Liv-ing, and as he lives I'll sing.

He lives/ hun-gry/ souls to\ feed,
Liv-ing to help in time of need.
Liv-ing to grant/ us/ rich\ sup\-ply,
Liv-ing to guide us with his eye.

He lives/ qui-et/-ing our\ fears,
Liv-ing to wipe a-way our tears,
Liv-ing to calm/ our/ troubl\-ed heart,
Liv-ing all bless-ings to im-part.

He lives/; glo-ry/ to his\ Name!
Liv-ing, my Je-sus, still the same.
Oh, sweet the joy/ this/ sen\-tence\ gives:
"I know that my Re-deem-er lives!"

Text: from Job 19:25-27, Samuel Medley, 1775, altered
Music: DUKE STREET, LM, John Hatton, 1793

Psalm 121

Antiphon *The Lord will keep you from all harm
and keep watch over your soul.*

I lift up my eyes to the mountains.
From where does my help come?
My help comes from the LORD,
Maker of heavens and earth,

Who will not let your foot slip
nor slumber when guarding you.
Indeed the guardian Israel
will not slumber and will not sleep.

The Lord is your guardian,
the Most High at your right hand.
By day the sun will not harm you,
nor the moon by the night.

The LORD will keep you from all harm
and guard your life.
The LORD will guard
your going and coming
from now and to forevermore.

*Glory to the Father, and to the Son,
and to the Holy Spirit*

As it was in the beginning, is now,
and will be for ever. Amen.

Antiphon　*The Lord will keep you from all harm
and keep watch over your soul.*

Psalm 130

Antiphon　*If you kept a record of sins,
Lord, who could stand?*

Out of the depths I cry to you, my LORD.
Lord, hear my voice.
Let your ears be attentive
to my cries for mercy.

If you kept a record of sins,
LORD, who could stand?
But with you is the forgiveness,
and so you are revered in awe.

Psalm 130, continued

I wait, my soul waits for the LORD,
in whose word I put hope.
My soul waits for the Lord
more than watchers for the morning,
even watchers for the morning.

Put hope, Israel, in the LORD!
For unfailing love is from the LORD,
in whom is full redemption,
who will redeem Israel from all their sins.

> *Glory to the Father, and to the Son,*
> *and to the Holy Spirit*

> As it was in the beginning, is now,
> and will be for ever. Amen.

Antiphon *If you kept a record of sins,*
Lord, who could stand?

CANTICLE

Philippians 2:6-11

Antiphon   *As the Father raises the dead,*
giving life,
so the Son gives life
to whom he wills.

Christ Jesus, subsisting in the form of God,
did not deem equality with God
    something to grab,
but emptied himself,
taking the form of a servant,
becoming in human likeness.

And being found in human fashion,
he humbled himself,
becoming obedient until death,
and death on a cross.

And so God highly exalted him,
and gave to him the name above every name,
that in the name of Jesus
every knee should bend,
of heavenly beings and earthly beings,
and beings under the earth;

Philippians 2:6-11, continued

And every tongue acknowledge
to the glory of God the Father
that Jesus Christ is Lord.

*Glory to the Father, and to the Son,
and to the Holy Spirit*

As it was in the beginning, is now,
and will be for ever. Amen.

Antiphon *As the Father raises the dead,
giving life,
so the Son gives life
to whom he wills.*

READING **1 Corinthians 15:51-57**

Brothers and sisters, I tell you a mystery:

We shall not all fall asleep, but we will all be changed, in an instant, in the blink of an eye, at the last trumpet. For the trumpet will sound and the dead will be raised incorruptible and we shall be changed. It is fitting for corruption to be clothed in incorruption and for the mortal to be clothed in immortality. And when the corruptible clothes itself in incorruption and the mortal clothes itself in immortality, then shall be the word that is written:

> *Death is swallowed up in victory.*
> *Where, O death, is your victory?*
> *Where, O death, is your sting?*

The sting of death is sin, and the power of sin is the law. But thanks be to God, giving to us the victory through our Lord Jesus Christ.

Responsory   from the *Te Deum*

In you, Lord, is our hope;
 - *our hope is not in vain.*

We shall dance and rejoice in your mercy;
 - *our hope is not in vain.*

Glory to the Father, and to the Son,
and to the Holy Spirit.
 - *In you, Lord, is our hope; our hope is not in vain.*

CANTICLE OF MARY   **Luke 1:46-55**

Antiphon   *All whom the Father gives me*
John 6:37   *will come to me and I will by no means*
                  cast out the one coming to me.

In Easter   *The crucified and risen Lord*
   Season   *has redeemed us, alleluia.*

+ My soul is stretched full with praise of the Lord,
  and my spirit, beyond joy in God, my Savior,
  who chose to lay eyes on this humble servant.

  Behold, now and forward,
  each and every age will call me blessed,
  for the Mighty One did great things to me.

  Holy is the name and the mercy
  to generations and generations,
  the ones fearing the One,

  Who scattered the haughty of mind and heart,
  pulled the powerful off their high place,
  and lifted with dignity the humble in need.

  The hungering are filled with good things,
  the rich are sent away empty,
  and servant Israel is given relief

with a memory of mercy to remember,
the promise spoken to our ancestors,
to Abraham and his descendants forever.

> *Glory to the Father, and to the Son,*
> *and to the Holy Spirit*

As it was in the beginning, is now,
and will be for ever. Amen.

Repeat antiphon.

INTERCESSIONS

Lord Jesus Christ, Son of the living God,
you raised your friend Lazarus from the dead;
- *raise all the dead you have redeemed.*

Christ, Consoler of those you healed
and those who loved them,
- *comfort all who mourn their dead.*

Christ, Savior and Redeemer of
the human family,
- *draw each of your brothers and sisters*
  into your loving mercy.

Christ, Giver of sight to the blind,
- *show yourself to those who do not know you.*

Christ, at length when sacraments shall cease,
- *welcome us to the heavenly banquet.*

Intercessions, continued

Eternal rest grant unto him/her/them, O Lord,
- *and let perpetual light shine upon him/her/them.*

May he/she/they rest in peace.
- *Amen.*

May his/her/their soul(s)
and the souls of all the faithful departed
through the mercy of God rest in peace.
- *Amen.*

And may the peace of God
which is beyond all human understanding
keep our minds and hearts
in the knowledge and love of God and of the Son,
our Lord and Savior Jesus Christ.
- *Amen.*

Our Fa-ther . . .

+ May the Lord bless us,
protect us from all evil,
and bring us to everlasting life. ***Amen.***

bedtime

Ho-ly God\, **we praise**/ **your Name**;
Lord of all\, we bow\ be-fore you!
All on earth\ your scep/-ter claim,
All in heav-en a-bove\ a-dore you;

   In-fin/-ite\ your vast do/-main,
   Ev-er-last\-ing is\ your reign.

Hark! the loud\ cel-es/-tial hymn
An-gel choirs\ a-bove\ are rais-ing,
Cher-u-bim\ and ser/-a-phim,
In un-ceas\-ing chor\-us prais-ing;

   Fill the/ heav-ens with sweet ac/-cord:
   Ho-ly, ho\-ly, ho\-ly Lord.

Ho-ly Fa\-ther, Ho/-ly Son,
Ho-ly Spir\-it, Three\ we name you;
While in ess\-ence on/-ly One,
Un-div-i\-ded God\ we claim you;

   And a/-dor\-ing bend the/ knee,
   While we en-ter the mys\-ter-y.

Text: Ignaz Franz, *GrosserGott*, about1774, tran. Clarence Walworth, 1858, altered
Music: 78 78 77 GROSSER GOTT, *Katholisches Gesangbuch, Vienna*, 1774

Psalm 91

Antiphon *Night holds no terrors for me*
sleeping in the shelter of God's wings.

One who dwells
in the shelter of the Most High,
in the shadow of Shaddai, will find rest.
I will say of my LORD,
my refuge, my fortress:
in my God do I trust.

Surely the Lord will save you
from fowler snare, from deadly pestilence.
With the feather of the Lord
you will be covered,
and under those wings you will find refuge,
shield and rampart,
the fidelity of the Lord.

You will have no fear of terror at night
nor of arrows flying by day,
of pestilence stalking in the darkness,
nor of plague that destroys at midday.

A thousand may fall at your side,
and ten thousand at your right hand;
near to you they will not come.

Observe with your eyes, simply watch;
punishment of doers of the bad you will see.
Make my LORD, who is my refuge,
make the Most High your dwelling.

Harm will not befall you,
nor will disaster come near your tent.
God's own Angels, the Lord will command
to guard you in all of your ways.

In their hands they will lift you up;
your foot will not strike against the stone.
Upon lion and cobra you will tread,
you will trample the great lion and serpent.

"Because you love me, I will rescue you,
I will protect all who know my Name.
You will call upon me and I will answer.
I am with you in trouble;
I will deliver you and honor you.

In length of days I will satisfy you,
and show you my salvation."

*Glory to the Father, and to the Son,
and to the Holy Spirit*

As it was in the beginning, is now,
and will be for ever. Amen.

Repeat antiphon.

READING **Revelation 22:1-5**

And the angel showed me a river of living water, sparkling as crystal, flowing out of the throne of God and of the Lamb, going through the middle of the street, and on either side of the river a tree of life producing twelve fruits, rendering the fruit of each month, and leaves of the tree as medicine for the nations.

Every curse will be no longer. The throne of God and of the Lamb will be in it, and his servants will worship him, and they will see his face, and his Name will be on their foreheads. Night will be no more, nor will they need lamplight or sunlight, for the Lord God will shine light on them and they will reign to forever and ever.

Responsory   Psalm 31:6

Into your hand, Lord,
- *I commend my spirit.*

You have redeemed us, Lord God of truth.
- *I commend my spirit.*

Glory to the Father, and to the Son,
and to the Holy Spirit.
- *Into your hand, Lord, I commend my spirit.*

CANTICLE OF SIMEON — Luke 2:29-32

Antiphon

Protect us, Lord, as we stay awake;
watch over us as we sleep,
that awake, we may keep watch with Christ,
and asleep, rest in his peace.
(alleluia)

+ Now, Lord, you set free your servant
according to your word in peace;
my eyes have seen your salvation,
which you have prepared
before the face of all the peoples,
a light for revelation to the nations
and glory for your people, Israel.

> *Glory to the Father, and to the Son,*
> *and to the Holy Spirit*

> As it was in the beginning, is now,
> and will be for ever. Amen.

Repeat antiphon.

✛ May the all-powerful Lord grant us
  a restful night and a peaceful death. ***Amen.***

HAIL MARY

Hail Mary, full of grace,
the Lord is with you.
Blessed are you among women,
and blessed is the fruit of your womb, Jesus.
Holy Mary, mother of God,
pray for us sinners,
now and at the hour of our death. ***Amen.***

middle *of the* night

A-ma-zing\ Grace! How sweet the sound
That saved a\ wretch like me.
I once\ was\ lost, but now/ am\ found,
Was blind, but\ now I see.

'**T**was grace that\ taught my heart to fear,
And grace my\ fears re-lieved.
How prec\-ious\ did that grace/ ap\-pear
The hour I\ first be-lieved.

Through ma-ny\ dan-gers, toils, and snares,
I have al\-rea-dy come.
'Tis grace\ hath\ brought me safe/ thus\ far,
And grace will\ lead me home.

When we've been\ there ten thou-sand years,
Bright shi-ning\ as the sun,
We've no\ less\ days to sing/ God's\ praise
Than when we'd\ first be-gun.

Text: John Newton, 1779
Music: NEW BRITAIN, CM, composer unknown;
Virginia Harmony, 1831

Psalm 40:2-14,17-18

Antiphon *You formed me, Lord, from the earth*
and clothed me with flesh;
be pleased, Lord,
to look on me and help me.

Waiting, I waited for the LORD,
who turned to me and heard my cry,

Who lifted me from the slime pit
and from the muddy mire,
and set my feet on rock,
making firm my standing place,

And put in my mouth a new song,
a hymn of praise to our God.
Many will see and fear and trust the LORD.

Blessed is the one who trusts in the LORD
and looks not to the proud
or those turning to false "gods."

LORD, my God,
many are your deeds of wonder
and your plans cannot be equaled.
Should I speak and tell of them
they would be too many to declare.

Sacrifice and offerings you did not desire,
but my ears you keep open for me.
Burnt offering and sin offering
you did not require.

Then I said, "Here, I have come;
In the scroll, in the book, it is written of me.
To do your will, my God, is my desire,
and your law is within my heart."

Your deed I proclaim in the great assembly.
See my lips unsealed; you, LORD, you know!

I do not hide in my heart what you do;
your faithfulness and your salvation I speak.
I do not conceal your love and your truth
from the great assembly.

Lord, withhold not your mercies from me,
may your love and your truth
protect me always
for countless troubles surround around me.

My sins overtake me and I cannot see.
They are more than the hairs of my head
and my heart fails me.

Be pleased, LORD, to save me;
LORD, come quickly to help me!...

Psalm 40:2-14,17-18, continued

May all who seek you rejoice in you and be glad
and may lovers of your salvation say always,
"Let God be exalted."

Yet I am poor and needy.
May the Lord think of me and not delay,
my help and my deliverer, my God.

> *Glory to the Father, and to the Son,*
> *and to the Holy Spirit*
>
> As it was in the beginning, is now,
> and will be for ever. Amen.

Antiphon   *You formed me, Lord, from the earth*
and clothed me with flesh;
be pleased, Lord,
to look on me and help me.

Psalm 42

Antiphon   *My soul thirsts for God,*
the living God; when may I go
and see the face of God?

As a deer breathes heavy for streams of water,
so my soul throbs for you, God.
My soul she thirsts for God, the living God.
When can I go and meet the faces of God?

My tears were food for me
by day and by night,
while all day they said to me,
"Where is your God?"

These things I remember
as my soul pours out before me:
How I would go with the multitude
to lead them to the house of God
sounding shouts of joy and thanksgiving,
a festive throng!

Why are you downcast, my soul?
Why are you disturbed within me?
Put hope in God, whom I will yet praise,
the saving help and presence.

My God, within me my soul she is downcast.
For this I will remember you
from the land of Jordan
and the heights of Hermon,
from the Mount of Mizar:

Deep calls to deep
in the roar of your waterfalls.
All your waves and breakers
are swept over me.

Psalm 42, continued

By day the LORD directs mercy
and at night the song within me
is a prayer to the God of my life.

I say to God my Rock,
"why do you forget me?
Why must I go about mourning,
oppressed by enmity?"

With mortal agony in my bones,
taunted by adversity,
while all day they say to me,
"Where is your God?"

Why are you downcast, my soul?
Why are you disturbed within me?
Put hope in God, whom I will yet praise,
my saving help and God.

> *Glory to the Father, and to the Son,
> and to the Holy Spirit*
>
> As it was in the beginning, is now,
> and will be for ever. Amen.

Antiphon *My soul thirsts for God,
the living God; when may I go
and see the face of God?*

READING **1 Corinthians 15:35-40**

Will someone say, *How are the dead raised?* or, *With what kind of body do they come?* Nonsense! What you sow does not come alive unless it dies. When sowing, you sow not the body that will become, but a naked seed, be it of wheat or corn or bean, but God gives it a body as God wishes, and to each of the seeds its own body. Not all flesh is the same, but one indeed of humans, and another flesh for animals, and another flesh for birds, and another for fishes. And there are heavenly bodies and earthly bodies.

Responsory Job 19:25,26,27

I know that my Redeemer lives
and on the last day I shall rise again.
 - *In my body I shall look on God, my Savior.*

My own eyes will gaze upon the Lord.
 - *In my body I shall look on God, my Savior.*

Glory to the Father, and to the Son,
and to the Holy Spirit.
 - *I know that my Redeemer lives
   and on the last day I shall rise again;
   in my body I shall look on God, my Savior.*

Let us bless the Lord. **Thanks be to God.**

www.ingramcontent.com/pod-product-compliance
Lightning Source LLC
Chambersburg PA
CBHW021200080526
44588CB00008B/429